Painting Heaven

Polishing the Mirror of the Heart

First published in 2014 by
Fons Vitae
49 Mockingbird Valley Drive
Louisville, KY 40207
http://www.fonsvitae.com
Email: fonsvitaeky@aol.com

Copyright Fons Vitae 2014

ISBN 978-1941610-13-8

Library of Congress Control Number 2014954219

Printed in China

Second printing, 2016

J
297
GHA

MARCH 2017

Painting Heaven

Polishing the Mirror of the Heart

BY

AL-GHAZALI,
DEMI AND
COLEMAN BARKS

ILLUSTRATED BY

Demi

From *Marvels of the Heart* by al-Ghazali

The story is told that once the Chinese and the Byzantines (Rūm) vied with one another before a certain king as to the beauty of their workmanship in decorating and painting. So the king decided to give over to them a portico so that the Chinese might decorate one side of it and the Byzantines the other side; and to let a curtain hang down between them so as to prevent either group from looking at the other. And he did so. The Byzantines gathered together countless strange colors, but the Chinese entered without any color at all and began to polish their side and to brighten it. When the Byzantines had finished, the Chinese claimed that they had finished also. The king was astonished at their statement and the way in which they had finished the decorating without any color at all. So they were asked, "How have you finished the work without any color?" They replied, "You are not responsible for us; lift the veil." So they lifted it, and behold on their side there shone forth the wonders of the Byzantine skill with added illumination and dazzling brilliance, since that side had become like unto a polished mirror by reason of much brightening. Thus the beauty of their side was increased by its added clearness.

The care of the saints in cleansing, polishing, purifying, and clarifying the heart until the true nature of the Real shines forth clearly therein with utmost illumination is like the work of the Chinese. The care of the learned and the philosophers in acquiring and adorning knowledge, and the representation of this adornment in the Heart, is like the work of the Byzantines.

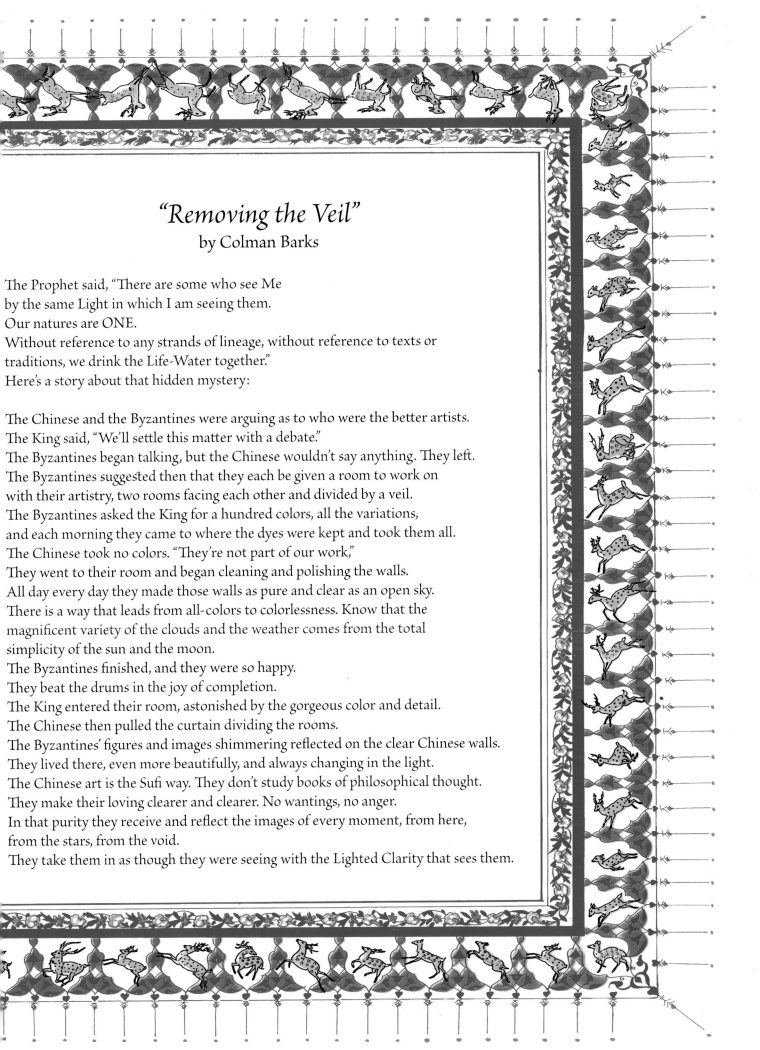

"Removing the Veil"
by Colman Barks

The Prophet said, "There are some who see Me
by the same Light in which I am seeing them.
Our natures are ONE.
Without reference to any strands of lineage, without reference to texts or
traditions, we drink the Life-Water together."
Here's a story about that hidden mystery:

The Chinese and the Byzantines were arguing as to who were the better artists.
The King said, "We'll settle this matter with a debate."
The Byzantines began talking, but the Chinese wouldn't say anything. They left.
The Byzantines suggested then that they each be given a room to work on
with their artistry, two rooms facing each other and divided by a veil.
The Byzantines asked the King for a hundred colors, all the variations,
and each morning they came to where the dyes were kept and took them all.
The Chinese took no colors. "They're not part of our work,"
They went to their room and began cleaning and polishing the walls.
All day every day they made those walls as pure and clear as an open sky.
There is a way that leads from all-colors to colorlessness. Know that the
magnificent variety of the clouds and the weather comes from the total
simplicity of the sun and the moon.
The Byzantines finished, and they were so happy.
They beat the drums in the joy of completion.
The King entered their room, astonished by the gorgeous color and detail.
The Chinese then pulled the curtain dividing the rooms.
The Byzantines' figures and images shimmering reflected on the clear Chinese walls.
They lived there, even more beautifully, and always changing in the light.
The Chinese art is the Sufi way. They don't study books of philosophical thought.
They make their loving clearer and clearer. No wantings, no anger.
In that purity they receive and reflect the images of every moment, from here,
from the stars, from the void.
They take them in as though they were seeing with the Lighted Clarity that sees them.

Once upon a time a Chinese man came to the court of the King. He said to the King, "I am a different and greater kind of artist because I can make heavenly paintings."

"My paintings contain all the colors of the rainbow, and also no colors at all; they contain all the clouds in the sky, the sun and the moon, the planets and stars and everything on earth; but they also contain Nothing at all but the shining Light of Heaven!"

The King of Persia thought this was very strange. He said, "We already have a great many wonderful painters here! However, if what you say is true, we will have a contest to decide the truth. I will give you six months to make your heavenly painting, and then I will choose the winner!"

The Chinese man agreed to the contest, and added, "I have just one condition: I must have a curtain that will veil my painting and not be removed until my painting is finished."

The King of Persia thought this was very strange too, but he agreed to the terms.

Then the king selected five of his very best painters for the contest. "You will have six months to make your paintings! I want you to do your very best, use all your imagination, creativity and power. I want you to use your very best paints too, for we don't want to be defeated by a foreigner! Good luck to you all!"

News spread throughout the land of the great painting contest. People wanted to come from every corner of the county to see the heavenly painting contest.

In the marketplace, people talked about the contest; they began packing their things to get ready to go and see the winner.

But the Byzantine painters were very worried. It seemed to them, too, that this Chinese man was very strange indeed, and so they asked the greatest astrologer in the land to read them their fortunes. Then they all prayed to the sun and the moon, the stars and the planets that they might win the contest.

The contest began. The Byzantine and the Chinese were each given a wall on which to paint that faced the opposite wall. However, as promised, there was a huge curtain veiling the entire space between the two works of art.

The Byzantine painters immediately began painting using the hundred colors of the rainbow. They painted the clouds in the sky, the sun and the moon, the planets and stars, children and animals, and everything on earth in perfect detail.

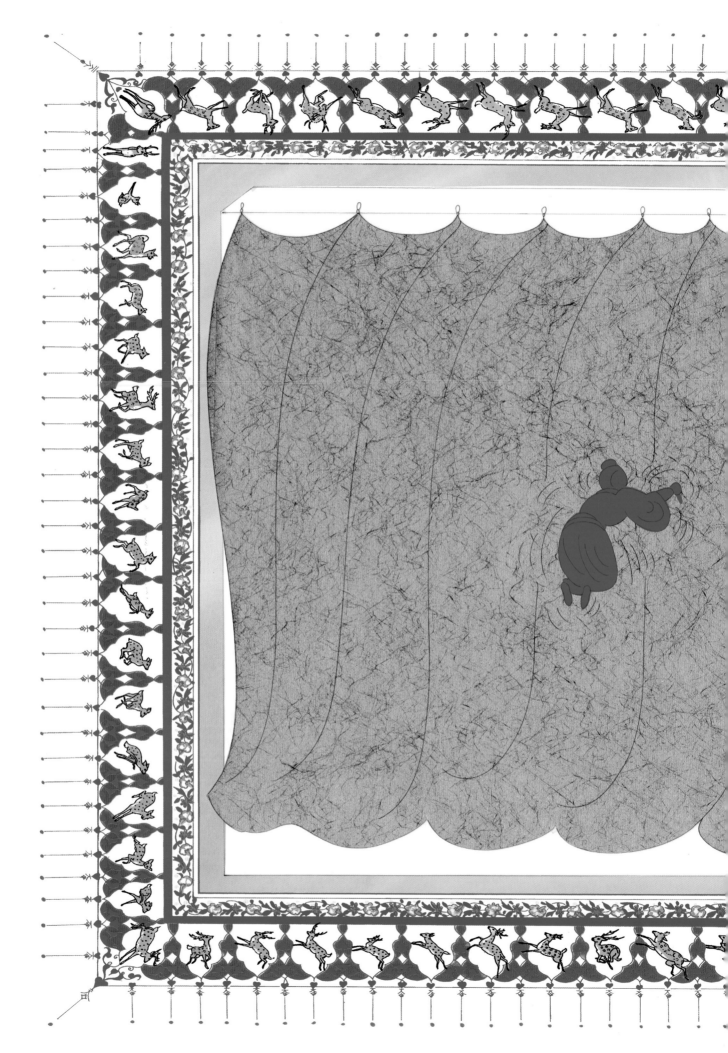

Now the Chinese man had asked for no colors at all. Neither had he asked for any brushes. He had only asked for polishing tools and cleaning rags! And it was also noticed that never did he have any paint spots on his hands or clothes. He would disappear in the morning behind his curtain, and reappear in the evening after working all day long. But what did he do? Nobody knew.

The King began to wonder if the Chinese man was crazy. He asked his doctor if this were so. His doctor replied, "A man is a little crazy if he paints in a painting contest, without any paints and without any brushes!"

Six months passed, and people were now all very excited. They gathered around the King when he declared, "The moment has come to decide the effort which is greater!"

The King first saw the painting of the Byzantines. He was so delighted by all the gorgeous colors, of the clouds in the sky, the sun and the moon, the planets and stars, the children and animals, and everything else on earth, that he jumped up and down and danced for joy shouting, "Bravo! Bravo! Beautiful! Beautiful! Well done!!"

But when the King pulled back the veil which had hidden the Chinese man's work of art, he was utterly astonished! He fell backwards onto the ground! Speechless! For there, on a pure polished wall with nothing on it at all, was reflected the Byzantine painting. It was far superior to the painted version. For now it was mirrored and shimmering, sparkling and shining, dazzling and enhanced, all by the Light of Heaven Truly this was a heavenly painting!

The King of Persia asked, "How have you done this magic? Are you a magician?" The Chinese man replied, "I am neither a magician nor a painter, but I am a humble monk. By polishing the wall for six months, I simply turned it into a mirror. I have made myself into a mirror too, for I have polished my Heart into a mirror for Heaven. Heaven is my Heart.

The King declared the Chinese man the winner. He said, "Those who polish their Hearts arrive at the Light. They can see, and reflect beauty directly at every moment. They have wiped away greed, envy, desire and hatred, and so those who paint with the Light of Heaven are always the winners in the end."

Then everyone celebrated and danced in the beautiful shimmering, sparkling, shining and dazzling light of the polished surface of the great heavenly painting!

Passages from The Marvels of The Heart
Book XXI of the *Ihya ulum al-din*
The Revival of the Religious Sciences
Fons Vitae 2005

Know that the seat (*maḥall*) of knowledge (*'ilm*) is the heart, by which I mean the subtle tenuous substance (*laṭīfa*) that rules all the parts of the body and is obeyed and served by all its members. In its relationship to the real nature of intelligibles (*ma'lūmāt*), it is like a mirror in its relationship to the forms (*ṣuwar*) of changing appearances (*mutalawwināt*). For even as that which changes has a form, and the image (*mithāl*) of that form is reflected in the mirror and represented therein, so also every intelligible has its specific nature, and this specific nature has a form that is reflected and made manifest in the mirror of the heart. Even as the mirror is one thing, the forms of individuals another, and the representation of their image in the mirror another, being thus three things in all, so here, too, there are three things: the heart, the specific natures of things, and the representation and presence of these in the heart. The 'intellect' (*al-'ālim*) is an expression for the heart in which there exists the image of the specific natures of things. The 'intelligible' (*al-ma'lūm*) is an expression for the specific natures of things. 'Intelligence' (*al-'ilm*) is an expression for the representation of the image in the mirror.

———————

So the comparison of [the heart] with the mirror is more apt, for man himself is not really present in the mirror, but there is present merely an image that corresponds to him, and thus the presence of an image in the heart corresponding to the real nature of the intelligible is called intelligence.

The mirror may not reflect the forms for five reasons: first, a defect in its formation, as, for example, a piece of crude iron before it is turned and shaped and polished; second, because of its dirt and rust and dullness, even though it is perfect in formation; third, because it is turned away from the direction of the object toward something else, as, for example, if the object were behind the mirror; fourth, because of a veil placed between the mirror and the object; and fifth, because of ignorance of the direction of the object desired, so that it is impossible to place it in front of the position and direction of the object.

Thus too is **the heart a mirror, ready to have reflected in it the true nature of reality in all things.** Hearts are destitute of the knowledge that they lack only because of the following five reasons.

The first reason is an imperfection in its own nature, such as the heart of a youth that does not reflect intelligibles because of its imperfection.

The second reason is because of dullness that is a result of acts of dis- obedience, and the filth from many lusts that are heaped upon the face of the heart, for these prevent the purity and cleanness of heart…

The third reason is that the heart may be turned away from the direction of reality which is sought. For the heart of the good and obedient man, although it is bright, does not have the clear statement of the Real revealed in it, for he does not seek the Real and does not have his mirror opposite to the direction of the thing sought. Perhaps all of his attention is taken up by the details of bodily submission or arranging the means of his livelihood, and his thought is not free to contemplate the Lordly Presence and the hidden divine realities. So there is revealed to him only that which he thinks about, whether it is the minute defects of his (religious) works or the hidden faults of the soul, if it is these which occupy his mind, or the interests of gaining a livelihood if he thinks of them. Now if limiting one's attention to works and the details of acts of obedience prevents the revelation of the clearness of the Real, what is your estimation (zann) of one who expends his energies in the lusts and pleasures of this present world and the things connected therewith and how should true revelation not be denied to such a person?

The fourth reason is the veil. The obedient man who has overcome his appetites and devotes himself exclusively to a certain specific reality may not have this revealed to him because it is veiled from him by some belief that he has held from his youth, and which he has blindly followed (taqlīd) and accepted in good faith. This belief walls him off from the true nature of the Real and prevents there being revealed to his heart anything contrary to the strict interpretation of the doctrines that he has blindly accepted. This too is a great veil that overshadows most Muslim theologians (mutakallimūn) and those who are zealous followers of the schools (madhāhib), and indeed most righteous men who think upon the kingdom of the heavens and the earth, for they are veiled by their blindly followed creeds that are hardened in their souls and firmly fixed in their hearts, and have become a veil between them and the perception of realities.

The fifth reason is ignorance of the direction from which the knowledge of the thing sought must be obtained. For the seeker after knowledge cannot obtain knowledge of that which is unknown except by recalling the knowledge that is related to what he desires, so that when he recalls it and arranges it within himself in a special order, to which the learned give the name of 'process of deduction' (tariq al-i-tibar), he will then have found the direction of the thing sought, and its true nature will be clearly revealed to his heart. For the things that are not instinctive, which one desires to know, cannot be caught save in the net of acquired knowledge; indeed no item of knowledge is acquired except from two preceding items of knowledge that are related and combined in a special way, and from their combination a third item of knowledge is gained. This is like the result of the union of a stallion and a mare. Here even as he who wishes to produce a mare cannot do so from donkey, cow, nor man, but from a special source, from male and female horses, and this if there takes place a special union; so also every item of knowledge has two special sources and a way for their combination, and from this combination there is gained the derived item of knowledge that is sought. Ignorance of these sources and of the inner aspect of combining them is what prevents understanding. An example of this already mentioned is the ignorance of the direction in which the object is.

The heart of every human being is, [in its original constitution], able and capable of bearing this trust, but the causes that we have mentioned prevent it from carrying this burden and arriving at the realization of the trust. In this connection the Prophet ﷺ said, "Every child is born with a natural conformity to religious truth (i.e., of Islam, *fiṭra*), and it is only his parents who make him a Jew or a Christian or a Magian…."

To this also is the reference in the *ḥadīth* that has come down from Ibn Umar ﷺ. He said, "The Messenger was asked, 'O Messenger of God, where is God in the earth or in heaven?' He replied, 'In the hearts of His believing creatures." There is also a narration [*ḥadīth qudsī*] that God, the Exalted, said, "My earth cannot

contain me, neither my heaven, but the tender and calm heart of my servant can contain Me."

Another narration says that the Messenger of God ﷺ was asked, "Who are the best of men?"

He replied, "Every believer whose heart is cleansed."

They asked, "What is the cleansed heart?"

He answered, "It is the Godfearing, pure heart, in which there is no fraud, nor iniquity, nor treachery, nor rancor, nor envy."

On that account Umar ﷺ said, "My heart saw my Lord when, because of Godly fear, He raised the veil." For whomsoever the veil is lifted between himself and God, the form of the material world (*al-mulk*) and of the world of spirits (*al-malakūt*) is clearly manifest in his heart, and he sees a Garden the width of a part of which is that of the heavens and the earth. Its total expanse is greater than the heavens and the earth, for 'the heavens and the earth' is only an expression for the visible material world, which, although broad in extent and far-reaching in compass, is still but a part of the whole. But the world of spirits is boundless, consisting of those secrets hidden from the sight of the eyes and perceived only by insight. It is true that only a part of it appears to the heart, but in itself and in its relation to the knowledge of God it is infinite. The material world and the world of spirits taken together under one classification are called the Lordly Presence (al-ḥaḍra al-rubūbiyya), for the Lordly Presence encompasses all existing things. For there exists nothing except God, the Exalted, His works, and His Kingdom; and His servants are a part of His works. What appears of this to the heart is, according to some, Paradise itself, and according to the people of reality (ahl al-ḥaqq), it is the means of deserving Paradise. The extent of his possession in Paradise is in proportion to the extent of his knowledge and the measure to which God and His attributes and works have been revealed to him.

from Chapter Six

The true doctrine is that the heart has the capacity to have revealed in it the true nature of reality in all things. But this is prevented by the intervention of the five aforementioned causes. **These are as a veil that hangs down between the mirror of the heart and the Preserved Tablet** (al-lawḥ al-maḥfūẓ), which is engraved with all that God has decreed until the day of resurrection. The reflection of the real nature of knowledge from the mirror of the Tablet upon the mirror of the heart is like the reflection of an image from one mirror to another mirror opposite it. The veil between the two mirrors is sometimes removed by the hand, and at other times by a gust of wind that moves it. Thus the winds of divine favor sometimes blow and the veils are drawn aside from the eyes of hearts so that there is reflected in

them something of that which is written upon the Preserved Tablet. Sometimes this takes place during sleep, and thereby there is revealed (yuʿlim) that which will come into being in the future. The veil is completely lifted by death, when the covering is withdrawn. At other times [inspiration] is made during waking hours and the veil is lifted by a secret favor from God, the Exalted, and some of the marvels of knowledge glisten in the heart from behind the curtain of the unknown. This may be like a dazzling flash of lightning, or it may be continuous up to a certain point, but its continuance is most rare. Inspiration (ilhām) then does not differ from acquisition as regards the knowledge itself, its seat, and its cause, but it differs only in the removal of the veil, for this is not accomplished by man's volition. General inspiration does not differ from prophetic inspiration in any of these respects, but only in the matter of the vision of the angel who imparts the knowledge; for our hearts attain knowledge only by means of the angels. To this the Exalted refers in the statement, *And it is not for any human being that God should speak to him except by revelation or from behind a partition or that He sends a messenger to reveal, by His permission, what He wills (42:51)…*

When God becomes the ruler of the heart, He floods it with mercy and sheds His light upon it, and the breast is opened and there is revealed to it the secret of the world of spirits (malakūt), and by a gift of mercy there is cleared away from the surface of the heart the veil of whiteness that blinds its eye, and there shines in it the real nature of divine things.

from Chapter Eight

Know that the wonders of the heart are outside the realm of things perceived through the senses (*mudrakāt al-ḥawāss*), for the heart is also beyond sense perception. The understandings are too weak to grasp, except by means of a tangible example, that which is not perceived through the senses. So we shall explain this to people of weak understanding by means of two examples.

For the first illustration let us suppose that a reservoir is dug in the earth, into which the water can be conducted from the surface above through streams which empty into it. The bed of the reservoir may also be dug up and the dirt removed from it until the fountain of pure water is reached, and then the water bursts forth from the bottom of the reservoir. This water is purer and more constant, and perhaps more copious and abundant. The heart then is like the reservoir and knowledge like the water. The five external senses are like the streams. Knowledge may possibly be conducted to the heart by means of the streams of the senses and the consideration of things observed until it is thus filled with knowledge. It is also possible to stop up these streams [from flowing into] it by solitude and seclusion and averting the eyes from seeing, and then to resolve in the depths of the heart to purify it and remove from it the layers of veils until the fountain of knowledge bursts forth from within it.

But if you say, "How can knowledge burst forth from the heart itself while it is destitute of it," know that this is one of the wonders of the heart's secrets. It is not permissible to deal with it in the knowledge of proper conduct (*'ilm al-mu'āmala*). This much, however, can be mentioned, that the real natures of things are written down in the Preserved Tablet (*al-lawḥ al-maḥfūẓ*), and indeed in the hearts of the angels who are brought near [to God].

For just as an architect draws plans for buildings on blank paper and then brings them into actuality in accordance with that archetype (*nuskha*), thus the creator of the heavens and the earth wrote an archetype of the world from beginning to end upon the Preserved Tablet, and then brought it into actuality in accordance with that archetype.

From the world which has been brought into actuality in the image [of the archetype] there is transmitted to the external senses and the retentive imagination (*khayāl*) still another image. For whoever looks at the sky and the earth and then closes his eyes, sees in his imagination the image of the sky and the earth, so that it is as though he were looking at them; and were the sky and the earth annihilated and he himself remained, he would find within himself the image of the sky and the earth as though he were beholding them and looking at them.

Then from his imagination an effect is transmitted to the heart, so that there is represented in it the real natures of things that have entered into sensation and imagination. The representation in the heart corresponds to the world that is represented in the imagination, which in turn corresponds to the world as it exists in itself, external to the imagination and heart of man. This existing world corresponds to the archetype existing in the Preserved Tablet.

Thus the world has four degrees of existence. There is existence in the Preserved Tablet; this is prior to its corporeal (*jismānī*) existence. Its real (*ḥaqīqī*) existence follows this, and it is followed in turn by its imaginative (*khayālī*) existence, by which I mean the existence of its image in the imagination. Its imaginative existence is followed by its intellectual existence, by which I mean the existence of its image within the heart. Some of these [orders of] being are immaterial (*rūḥāniyya*) and some [are] corporeal. Of the immaterial, some are more immaterial in their [order of] being than others. This is a kindness (*luṭf*) coming from the divine wisdom; for God has made the pupil of your eye in such a way that, in spite of its smallness, there is pictured within it the image of the world, the heavens and the earth, with all their widespread extent. Then it goes on from existence in the realm of sensation to existence in the imagination, and from it to existence in the heart. For you can never apprehend anything save that which has reached you; and were it not that He has placed an image (*mithāl*) of the whole world within your very being you would have no knowledge of that which is apart from yourself. Glory belongs unto Him who has ordered these wonders in the heart and eye, and then blinded the heart and eye to the perception of them so that the hearts of the majority of creatures have become ignorant of themselves and their wonders.

Let us now go back to intended purpose and say, "It is conceivable that the real nature of the world might be represented in the heart, its mental image coming now from the senses and again from the Preserved Tablet; even as it is conceivable that the image of the sun should be represented in the eye, coming now from looking directly at it, and again from looking at the water on which the sun shines which reproduces its image." **So whenever the veils are lifted between the heart and the Preserved Tablet, the heart sees the things which are therein, and knowledge bursts forth into it therefrom, so that it does not have to acquire its knowledge through the avenues of the senses. This is like the bursting forth of water from the depths of the earth. Whenever the heart becomes occupied with things in the imagination derived from sensibles (*maḥsūsāt*), this veils it from examining the Preserved Tablet, just as when water is collected from streams [into a reservoir]; it is thereby prevented from bursting forth from the earth; or just as he who looks into the water that reproduces the image of the sun is not looking at the sun itself.**

Thus the heart has two doors. One door

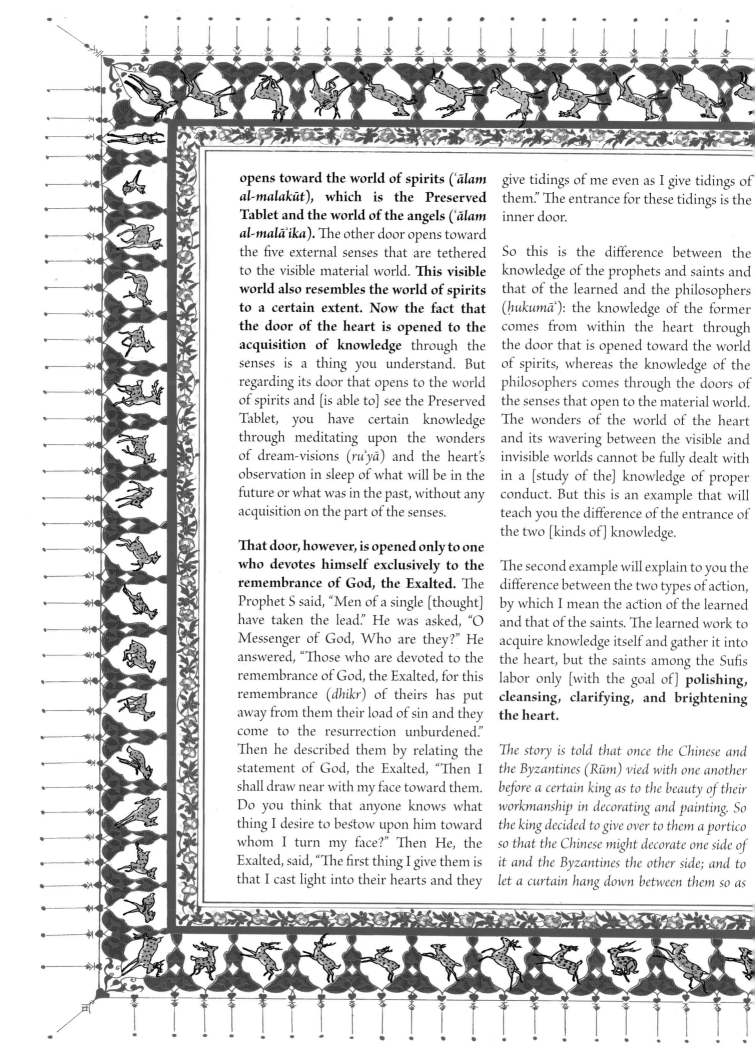

opens toward the world of spirits (**ʿālam al-malakūt**), which is the Preserved Tablet and the world of the angels (**ʿālam al-malāʾika**). The other door opens toward the five external senses that are tethered to the visible material world. **This visible world also resembles the world of spirits to a certain extent. Now the fact that the door of the heart is opened to the acquisition of knowledge** through the senses is a thing you understand. But regarding its door that opens to the world of spirits and [is able to] see the Preserved Tablet, you have certain knowledge through meditating upon the wonders of dream-visions (*ruʾyā*) and the heart's observation in sleep of what will be in the future or what was in the past, without any acquisition on the part of the senses.

That door, however, is opened only to one who devotes himself exclusively to the remembrance of God, the Exalted. The Prophet S said, "Men of a single [thought] have taken the lead." He was asked, "O Messenger of God, Who are they?" He answered, "Those who are devoted to the remembrance of God, the Exalted, for this remembrance (*dhikr*) of theirs has put away from them their load of sin and they come to the resurrection unburdened." Then he described them by relating the statement of God, the Exalted, "Then I shall draw near with my face toward them. Do you think that anyone knows what thing I desire to bestow upon him toward whom I turn my face?" Then He, the Exalted, said, "The first thing I give them is that I cast light into their hearts and they

give tidings of me even as I give tidings of them." The entrance for these tidings is the inner door.

So this is the difference between the knowledge of the prophets and saints and that of the learned and the philosophers (*ḥukumāʾ*): the knowledge of the former comes from within the heart through the door that is opened toward the world of spirits, whereas the knowledge of the philosophers comes through the doors of the senses that open to the material world. The wonders of the world of the heart and its wavering between the visible and invisible worlds cannot be fully dealt with in a [study of the] knowledge of proper conduct. But this is an example that will teach you the difference of the entrance of the two [kinds of] knowledge.

The second example will explain to you the difference between the two types of action, by which I mean the action of the learned and that of the saints. The learned work to acquire knowledge itself and gather it into the heart, but the saints among the Sufis labor only [with the goal of] **polishing, cleansing, clarifying, and brightening the heart.**

The story is told that once the Chinese and the Byzantines (Rūm) vied with one another before a certain king as to the beauty of their workmanship in decorating and painting. So the king decided to give over to them a portico so that the Chinese might decorate one side of it and the Byzantines the other side; and to let a curtain hang down between them so as to prevent either group from looking at the other. And he did so. The Byzantines gathered together countless strange colors, but the Chinese entered without any color at all and began to polish their side and to brighten it. When the Byzantines had finished, the Chinese claimed that they had finished also. The king was astonished at their statement and the way in which they had finished the decorating without any color at all. So they were asked, "How have you finished the work without any color?" They replied, "You are not responsible for us; lift the veil." So they lifted it, and behold on their side there shone forth the wonders of the Byzantine skill with added illumination and dazzling brilliance, since that side had become like unto a polished mirror by reason of much brightening. Thus the beauty of their side was increased by its added clearness.

The care of the saints in cleansing, polishing, purifying, and clarifying the heart until the true nature of the Real shines forth clearly therein with utmost illumination is like the work of the Chinese. The care of the learned and the philosophers in acquiring and adorning knowledge, and the representation of this adornment in the heart, is like the work of the Byzantines.

But whatever the [truth] of this matter, the heart of the believer does not die, nor is its knowledge erased at death nor its clearness clouded. To this Ḥasan, may God have mercy on him, referred in his saying, "Dust will not consume the seat of faith." This knowledge is a means of access that brings him near to God, the Exalted. But

what [the heart] has attained of knowledge itself; or what it has attained of purity and the capacity to receive what knowledge writes upon the heart, does not enable it to dispense with more knowledge. There is no happiness for anyone, apart from learning and mystical knowledge and some degrees of happiness are more noble than others...
from Chapter Nine

This was the meaning of the saying of [the Prophet] ﷺ, "Verily there are in my nation recipients of discourse, and Umar is one of them."

There is a tradition (*athar*) that God, the Exalted, says, "Whenever I examine the heart of a man and find persistent remembrance of Me pre- ponderant therein, I assume control over him and become his companion; I converse with him and become his familiar friend." Abū Sulaymān al-Dārānī, may God's mercy be upon him, said, "The heart is like a pavilion that has been pitched, around which are closed doors, and whatever door is opened onto it influences it."

So it appears that the opening of one of the doors of the heart is toward the world of spirits and the highest beings. This door is opened by means of striving, scrupulous piety (*waraʿ*), and shunning the lusts of this present world. For this reason Umar ؓ wrote to the commanders of the troops, "Remember what you hear from those who are obedient [to God] for they have inspirations that are true."